# A Letter

# to the

# Maker of Laws

## (A Stage Play)

Rubaba Mmahajia Rahma Sabtiu

Rubaba Mmahajia Rahma Sabtiu

# A Letter to the Maker of Laws (A Stage Play)

## <u>CONTENT PAGE</u>

# ACKNOWLEDGEMENT

I am most grateful to God for everything. My heart felt gratitude to all those who helped me in writing and publishing this book in any way. May God bless you all.

# DEDICATION

*To the service of God Almighty*

*To my Irreplaceable mum*

*To my Family & Friends*

*To my mentors*

*& to*

# *YOU*

# DISCLAIMER

All characters in this play are fictitious. Any resemblance to real persons, living or dead, is purely coincidental. I apologise if this play was unable to deliver the message in the most perfect manner to everyone. May God forgive me for any mistakes and accept my efforts. Please pray for all those who worked hard for this to become a reality. This play should not be staged without the prior permission of the author.

*By the author*

# A Letter to the Maker of Law
## (A poem)

When a little girl decides to speak to the elderly

The elderly that would not listen even to their fellow elders

When she wants to take advantage of her innocent mind

To narrate to the high and mighty a story

A story of the suffering of a people to whom she belongs

When she cannot find the right means

Yet she cannot keep her worries to herself

When she finds a means she could use at least

And she calls it a letter

A letter she intends to give to the maker of laws

But she worries for her choice of language

She worries for her choice of words

Will the maker of laws find it offensive?

Will the maker of laws even understand her?

And will the maker of laws take action?

Yet she writes her worries down

She could not settle for silence

For to her that is equal to cowardice

# THE CAST

**FATIMATU ZAHRA:**

An intelligent fifteen year old daughter of Mma Safia Nurse and Lawyer Musa

**MMA SAFIA NURSE:**

A nurse whose dress code as a Muslim woman is not accepted in the hospital where she works

**LAWYER MUSA:**

A vibrant and popular lawyer

**ENGLISH TEACHER:**

Fatimatu Zahra's English teacher who detests her religion

**PATRICK:**

Fatimatu Zahra's school mate

**HAMIDA:**

Fatimatu Zahra's cousin

**MR. YAHYA NABIL:**

Lawyer Musa's friend and Hamida's husband

**KRAMO:**

An inhabitant of Lawyer Musa's house

**THE NARRATOR**

# A Letter to the Maker of Laws (A Stage Play)

PLAY BEGINS...

*[Stage opens with Fatimatu Zahra sitting on a chair with a table in front of her. On the table is a sheet of paper and a pen. She sits quietly and stares at the things on the table. The Narrator enters quietly and comes to stand a little away from her]*

**NARRATOR:**

*(Staring at her, she turns to the audience)* Grieve fills her heart. She thinks but she can't understand. A little girl, barely sixteen years. In her own way, she tries to get her sorrow into words *(she exits).*

**FATIMATU ZAHRA:**

*(She picks the pen and looks at the audience)* How would they understand my language? What words should I use? How should I say it? Oh God! Give me the wisdom to do this. Give me the courage to relate my worry. To whom do I address my statements? *(She is about to write but she stops)* To Whom It May Concern is not good *(She closes her eyes and puts her forehead on the table. The Narrator enters quietly again).*

**NARRATOR:**

*(To the audience)* To Whom It May Concern is not good. Nobody would be concerned. Not me nor anyone. But even if it is you and I, what help could we possibly offer her? We can only share in her opinion. *(She turns to Fatimatu Zahra then she looks up)* Oh Allah! Give her the wisdom to know who really would be concerned *(She exits and Fatimatu Zahra raises her head).*

Rubaba Mmahajia Rahma Sabtiu

**FATIMATU ZAHRA:**

*(Smiling)* Yes! It should be him or her. In his or her hands lies the power in this worldly life, to make the laws. *(She begins to write).*

Post Office Box, 5555

Ghana *(She pauses)*

The Maker of Laws

Wherever you are

Dear Sir/Madam

### AN APPEAL FROM THE CORE OF MY HEART

*(She stops and looks up and then she continues)* Oh Maker of Laws! Forgive me if I have skipped protocol. I have an great respect for your office and my little mind tells me that you are the one who would be concerned as well as be able to help me. At age fifteen and almost sixteen, I have a lot of requests to ask of you. My letter might be very long. *(She stops and puts her forehead on the table. The Narrator enters)*

**NARRATOR:**

*(To the audience)* An apology to the Maker of Laws. The one she thinks would be concerned. The one she believes could help a little girl out of her plight. Is that really so? Well, her words are going to be lengthy, she cautions. *(She heaves a sigh)* Her first worry, she relates. *(She exits)*

## A Letter to the Maker of Laws (A Stage Play)

**FATIMATU ZAHRA:**

*(She lifts her head and begins to write)* Oh Maker of Laws! My foremost request is my mother. She is a nurse and… *(Lights go out on stage and come on again with Mma Safia Nurse and Fatimatu Zahra on stage)*

**MMA SAFIA NURSE:**

*(Holding Fatimatu Zahra's hand)* My dear, please take very good care of yourself. Your dad would be with you soon, ok.

**FATIMATU ZAHRA:**

I'll do that mum. Have a nice day.

**MMA SAFIA NURSE:**

Thank you. *(She begins to walk out and Fatimatu Zahra stares at her)*

**FATIMATU ZAHRA:**

*(Loudly)* Mum?

**MMA SAFIA NURSE:**

*(Turning)* Yes.

**FATIMATU ZAHRA:**

Do you have to take off your Hijab at work?

**MMA SAFIA NURSE:**

*(Saddened, she comes closer to her)* I have no option my dear. My job demands it.

**FATIMATU ZAHRA:**

But why should that be? Don't you have a right to cover yourself?

**MMA SAFIA NURSE:**

There are so many things that you cannot understand now.

**FATIMATU ZAHRA:**

Don't I know the difference between wrong and right?

**MMA SAFIA NURSE:**

At your age, I sometimes wonder how you could be this intelligent but you have to know that the world especially this country doesn't always work in our favour.

**FATIMATU ZAHRA:**

But why are your uniforms strictly that style?

**MMA SAFIA NURSE:**

They talk about smartness.

**FATIMATU ZAHRA:**

Smartness? The men wear trousers and long sleeve shirts. Isn't that almost-Hijab? Aren't they smarter and safer in that? Couldn't the Muslim women nurses be allowed their uniform in that style at least?

**MMA SAFIA NURSE:**

Hmmm! If only I could answer those intelligent questions you are asking.

**FATIMATU ZAHRA:**

But mum, don't you have the right to worship?

## A Letter to the Maker of Laws (A Stage Play)

**MMA SAFIA NURSE:**

That, my dear, is the longest story I have ever heard. I don't sometimes understand what that statement means in some cases.

**FATIMATU ZAHRA:**

But what harm would such a dress cause?

**MMA SAFIA NURSE:**

It is amazing my dear. Very amazing!

**FATIMATU ZAHRA:**

Why do surgeons cover their whole body during surgery?

**MMA SAFIA NURSE:**

To prevent infection. The Hijab could do the hospital a lot of good but who will understand?

**FATIMATU ZAHRA:**

Can't you fight for your right, mum?

**MMA SAFIA NURSE:**

*(She heaves a sigh)* I have done and I'm still doing my best. It is very hard for one person to do all these things. Other nurses who are Muslims do not care about it. They even love it. So you see, it is not an easy task at all.

**FATIMATU ZAHRA:**

But why are you the only one? Why aren't the other Muslims bothered?

**MMA SAFIA NURSE:**

You know, some of us have chosen to be liberal about the rules of Islam. It is like a conflict between us and the religion we claim to be following. Sometimes I wish I could quit and do something else but I want to be a part of the life-saving team. Besides, our Muslim women need their fellow Muslim women in that sector to see to them. Insha'a Allah, I'll continue to fight for that but for now, we have to manage it as it is.

**FATIMATU ZAHRA:**

*(She stares sadly at Mma Safia Nurse)* I wish I could help. If only I was older mum.

**MMA SAFIA NURSE:**

*(She hugs her)* Oh my darling angel! You have done your part by your wisdom-filled questions and I know that if you grow up, God will help you to do something. *(She begins to leave)*

**FATIMATU ZAHRA:**

*(Smiling)* All the best for you and your patients.

**MMA SAFIA NURSE:**

Thank you *(She blows a kiss to her and Fatimatu Zahra does the same then she exits).*

**FATIMATU ZAHRA:**

*(To the audience)* If only I had the power! If only I was older! If only I was richer and stronger! If only… *(She looks up)* Oh Allah! What can I do whiles I am young? *(Lights go*

out and come on with Fatimatu Zahra by the desk as before. She puts her forehead on the table again and the Narrator enters)

**NARRATOR:**

(To the audience) If only this! If only that! What can she do whiles she is as she is? (She points to Fatimatu Zahra) But why must she worry? After all, is she not a little girl? (She exits and Fatimatu Zahra raises her head)

**FATIMATU ZAHRA:**

(She begins to write) In our Holy Book lies a command from God for us to cover our whole body leaving our faces and hands for tangible reasons. Oh Maker of Laws! My mum and many others are deprived of this right due to their jobs. In the laws lie freedom of worship. If you really mean it, then please answer to the call of this faint voice. The same uniform sewn to suit the Hijab. It can be done Oh Maker of Laws! It can be done. (She puts her head on the table and lifts it up again)

My second request is me and others like me. (Lights go out and come on with Fatimatu Zahra walking from one end of the stage towards the other with a bag strapped behind her. When she gets to the centre, English Teacher comes from the other side and stood staring at her)

**FATIMATU ZAHRA:**

(She sees him and she starts smiling) Good Morning English Teacher.

**ENGLISH TEACHER:**

(Staring at her disgustingly) What are you wearing?

Rubaba Mmahajia Rahma Sabtiu

**FATIMATU ZAHRA:**

*(She looks at herself)* What?

**ENGLISH TEACHER:**

Are you not supposed to be in your school uniform?

**FATIMATU ZAHRA:**

*(Politely)* I am in my uniform sir. I'll take this *(She points to her dress)* off when I get to the school's entrance.

**ENGLISH TEACHER:**

Why should a nice and very intelligent girl like you dress like an old woman? From today onwards, I don't want to ever see you in that *(He points to her dress)*.

**FATIMATU ZAHRA:**

How do you mean sir?

**ENGLISH TEACHER:**

I mean what I said. If you want to live in peace in the school then you better obey this simple rule. The teachers have been saying it but I never believed them if not for today.

**FATIMATU ZAHRA:**

I really don't see what I have done wrong. Don't I have the right to dress the way I want outside school? I have never worn this in school anyway.

## A Letter to the Maker of Laws (A Stage Play)

**ENGLISH TEACHER:**

One more thing, you better tell those your Muslim friends that whether Eid or not, they are staying in school and also tell the Muslims who are day students that I want to conduct a test on the morning of that day. If you don't come, you will surely fail *(He exits).*

**FATIMATU ZAHRA:**

*(Dumb-founded)* But? What? Could you imagine? What is this man trying to say? And does he think we would just fold our arms over our chests in submission to his will? He's joking indeed. *(Lights go out and come on with her seated as before)*

Oh Maker of Laws! That is the attitude of some of them to us. Our freedom is nonsense to them. They attack us emotionally knowing our insignificant number in their schools. Aren't they public schools? Don't we Muslims have the right to public schools? *(Lights go out on stage again and come on with Fatimatu Zahra's hands on her waist angrily. Patrick enters without her notice)*

**PATRICK:**

Hello Fatimatu Zahra! *(She turns to him and she smiles)*

**FATIMATU ZAHRA:**

Hi Patrick!

**PATRICK:**

Why are you always so early to school?

**FATIMATU ZAHRA:**

But you are also early, aren't you?

**PATRICK:**

I have a special agenda today that is why.

**FATIMATU ZAHRA:**

Let us go together then *(She begins to move).*

**PATRICK:**

Stop. *(She stops)* Did you hear about what happened in school Last Friday?

**FATIMATU ZAHRA:**

No, I didn't. What happened?

**PATRICK:**

I decided to stay after school for a while before going home and we heard that one teacher was punishing one of the Muslim students for praying in the dormitory.

**FATIMATU ZAHRA:**

*(Surprised)* What? Who was that?

**PATRICK:**

When we went to the dormitory, we realized it was their housemistress who had punished him.

**FATIMATU ZAHRA:**

Who was she punishing?

## A Letter to the Maker of Laws (A Stage Play)

**PATRICK:**

Alhassan, the boy who had the most disciplined student award for the form twos this year.

**FATIMATU ZAHRA:**

Why did she punish him? Was he to do something else at that time?

**PATRICK:**

Not at all. School had closed and I learnt one of the dorm mates went to report him to her.

**FATIMATU ZAHRA:**

But are they not allowed to pray in their dorms?

**PATRICK:**

Some of the teachers don't allow that in the Hostels.

**FATIMATU ZAHRA:**

*(Annoyed)* Look Patrick. Say no more. Let's get to school. I want to find out what happened myself. *(They exit. Lights go out and come on with Fatimatu Zahra seated as before. She begins to write)*

And it is true oh Maker of Laws! That is the agony some of them subject us to. What harm does a less than five-minutes of silent prayer cause to the activities of a school? They tell us, 'Go to Islamic schools if you want to practice Islam?' They hit us where it hurts most knowing our weaknesses. Please hear my far away cry Oh Maker of Laws!

My third request to many might be insignificant but indispensable to a Muslim. My cousin, an admirable intelligent young lady and her challenges. *(Lights go out on stage and come on with Fatimatu Zahra seated on a prayer mat and reading a Qur'an. Hamida enters and goes to sit on a chair beside Fatimatu Zahra)*

**HAMIDA:**

*(Looking worried)* Hi sweetest cousin! The peace and mercy of Allah be with you *(She smiles).*

**FATIMATU ZAHRA:**

*(She stops reading and she turns to Hamida smiling)* Ameen! And may the same be with you precious one. *(They hold hands)* How was your day?

**HAMIDA:**

Alhamdu lil laah. In all things we give thanks to God.

**FATIMATU ZAHRA:**

You don't look too happy. Didn't you get the job again?

**HAMIDA:**

Sure, I didn't. They all want me to take off my veil.

**FATIMATU ZAHRA:**

I really don't understand them at all. Don't Muslims patronize their services too?

## A Letter to the Maker of Laws (A Stage Play)

**HAMIDA:**

Ask that again. They tell me that they would love to have me among their employees because I have a wonderful personality and a great qualification but... *(She pauses)*

**FATIMATU ZAHRA:**

But your hijab

**HAMIDA:**

*(She nods)* I know I will surely get a great job insha'a Allah but I feel hurt because most of the Muslim ladies I know accept their terms of offer so easily and some don't even want to do the Hijab even if they are allowed to.

**FATIMATU ZAHRA:**

It is painful indeed

**HAMIDA:**

Can you imagine what one man actually told me today? He said that they needed my feminine features on the job meanwhile it is not a modelling agency.

**FATIMATU ZAHRA:**

That is disgusting

**HAMIDA:**

That is the last thing I need and want. I'm really going to do something about that insha'a Allah. *(Lights go out and come on with Fatimatu Zahra seated as before and she writes)*

**FATIMATU ZAHRA:**

And now, she has a great job that respects her principles as a Muslim. A job that has termed her the best and most well-paid employee but the reality in our environment still remains the same. Majority of them throw us away for such a trivial reason thereby depriving us of our right to work and earn a living as Muslims. *(She stands up and walks to one end of the stage and she begins to sing)*

Lord! I am just a little girl. Trying hard to understand. Where is our place in their plans O Lord! Help this girl. It's time. Like a grain of sand, slipping through the palm of my hands, I realize, I need to write this *(She points to the letter on the table)*. Oh Lord! Help this girl! Help me! So many things I have to write. They come fleeting by as I write and I wonder, how merciful can they be oh Lord! Help me! *(She goes to sit down and the Narrator enters slowly as she puts her head on the table)*.

**NARRATOR:**

Why would a girl so little bother herself with a task so huge? When we were children, we were never bothered. As adults, we were not bothered and as old men and women, we were not bothered. We died without bothering. In the past, we were not bothered and in our present life, we are not bothered and it doesn't look like we will ever bother. But here is a little girl bothering *(She pauses)*. Oh Fatimatu Zahra! Where from this blazing passion? *(Lights go out and come on with Mma Safia Nurse sitting on a mat and reading)*.

# A Letter to the Maker of Laws (A Stage Play)

**MMA SAFIA NURSE:**

*(Looking in the book)* I need to go and rest for a while. *(Lawyer Musa comes in and she sees him)* You are welcome my husband.

**LAWYER MUSA:**

*(He smiles)* Thank you my wife. Assalaamu alaikum.

**MMA SAFIA NURSE:**

Wa alaikum salaam. *(He sits on a chair close by)* You look stressed out.

**LAWYER MUSA:**

It was not as easy as I thought. Where is my princess anyway?

**MMA SAFIA NURSE:**

She is in the study.

**LAWYER MUSA:**

I'm sure she's not done with her words to the Owner of the Universe yet.

**MMA SAFIA NURSE:**

*(Laughing)* Is that what she told you she was writing?

**LAWYER MUSA:**

I cannot really remember but it sounds like that I guess.

**MMA SAFIA NURSE:**

She calls it; "A Letter to the Maker of Laws."

**LAWYER MUSA:**

*(Nodding)* Ok. I remember those words. A very interesting girl with an interesting agenda.

**MMA SAFIA NURSE:**

We should thank God for this angel of a daughter *(Fatimatu Zahra enters and she goes to sit beside her mother).*

**FATIMATU ZAHRA:**

*(To Lawyer Musa)* Daddy, welcome.

**LAWYER MUSA:**

Thank you my dear. I was just asking of you.

**FATIMATU ZAHRA:**

You took very long

**LAWYER MUSA:**

The problem was not as simple as I thought Zahra. I think you should include it in your letter.

**MMA SAFIA NURSE:**

*(Smiling)* I think you two can kindly go and talk about this somewhere else. I would hear from you later but for now, I have to finish this *(She lifts the book up).*

## A Letter to the Maker of Laws (A Stage Play)

**LAWYER MUSA:**

*(He stands up)* All right! Point well noted. Sweetie, let's go talk human rights *(Fatimatu Zahra stands up and follows him).*

**FATIMATU ZAHRA:**

*(Turning to her mother)* Mummy, could I accompany you to court the next time you go there please?

**MMA SAFIA NURSE:**

I will more than love that.

**FATIMATU ZAHRA:**

*(Happily)* Thank you mum *(They exit).*

**MMA SAFIA NURSE:**

*(To the audience)* Who will not want a person like my daughter standing by her as she tries to be heard and given some practical freedom? *(She pauses)* She wants to fight but where lies her strength? A piece of paper? Ink from a pen? Words so faint? A combination that never gets anywhere close to the table of the makers of laws? *(She looks up and back at the audience)* But Allah appreciates those little efforts even if it doesn't get us anywhere *(Lights go out and come on with Hamida seated on a chair and staring at the audience).*

**HAMIDA:**

*(She puts her hand to her jaw and sings)* Allah Allah Yaa Allah! Allah Allah Yaa Allah! My life is empty without you. Nothing I've gained is without you. If you are pleased, my

soul can breathe. Where will I be without you? My heart now flees this worldly dream.

Yearning for mercy from you *(Fatimatu Zahra enters and starts singing).*

**FATIMATU ZAHRA:**

*(Pacing the stage)* Now I realize. I was so unwise. Abandoned his advice. Shame on me.

Help was always near if we persevere. If we held on just for a while. *(They all laugh and*

*Fatimatu Zahra comes to sit beside Hamida as Narrator enters and starts singing)*

**NARRATOR:**

Don't you worry. Follow the signs. Leave the story to the Divine. Free yourself by

saying what's true. Be yourself though it may be hard *(She exits. Hamida and Fatimatu*

*Zahra hug each other happily).*

**HAMIDA:**

It is good to have you here Fatima. I needed someone to talk to and though you are

young, I think you are the best person to talk to.

**FATIMATU ZAHRA:**

*(She pulls a mat and sits on it in front of Hamida)* What is going on with you? I'm all ears.

**HAMIDA:**

I just hope you will include it in your letter.

**FATIMATU ZAHRA:**

*(They laugh)* Insha'a Allah, I will. *(Lights go out and come on again with Fatimatu Zahra at*

*the desk and she begins to write)* My father's new case oh Maker of Laws, is a great

26

headache. A non-Muslim employer and his Muslim employee. The employee as usual decides to pray during his break time. The employer decides to sack him for praying whiles at work. Unfair indeed is this. Didn't he hire him as a Muslim? What harm does praying in an obscene corner of an office during break time cause to an enterprise? Yet the court wants to rule in his favour because he has influence. Oh Maker of Laws! What does this mean? *(She stands up and comes to sit cross-legged in front of the audience)* And to my cousin, they tell; "Don't let Islam oppress you! You are too good to be hidden behind a veil." And then she tries to explain to them but they never understand. If only they knew, the essence of Islam to a person who understands Islam. But no! They never learn and they never stop saying lies and holding unto misconceptions like their lives depended on it *(She becomes motionless and the Narrator enters)*.

**NARRATOR:**

*(She begins to sing)* The heart of a Muslim is sincere. And the heart of a Muslim must be strong. It is the heart of a Muslim through the guidance of Islam that makes you fair and kind and helpful to your fellow men. So living as a Muslim means that you must play a part. Allah looks not at how you look but what is in your heart. *(Fatimatu Zahra comes into motion and the Narrator stares at her as she continue singing)* It is time you should know. You will learn as you grow that some people around, will do their best to bring you down but you have to be a star that shines so bright for the heart of a Muslim does what's right *(Fatimatu Zahra smiles and goes back to the desk. Narrator stares at her and starts*

*singing again as she sits down)* So whatever you do, make sure you are with the truth. Honesty is the best because life is a test even if it hurts so much you want to cry. Remember the heart of a Muslim is sincere *(Fatimatu Zahra smiles and puts her head on the table. Narrator stares at her happily for a while and she exits. Lights go out and come on with English Teacher and Mr Yahya Nabil arguing).*

**ENGLISH TEACHER:**

*(Angrily)* You think you can just come here and tell me nonsense?

**MR YAHYA NABIL:**

You better be careful with your attitude towards the Muslim students or else I will put you behind bars one day.

**ENGLISH TEACHER:**

You are joking. Build schools and keep them there if you want them to practise that barbaric religion you call Islam. So far as they are in the school I teach, they can't practise Islam when I am around period.

**MR YAHYA NABIL:**

*(Calmly)* What do you have against Islam?

**ENGLISH TEACHER:**

And you expect me to answer that? I don't deal with rowdy people if you care to know.

**MR YAHYA NABIL:**

*(Angrily)* Mind your words my friend. You have no idea whom you are talking to.

## A Letter to the Maker of Laws (A Stage Play)

**ENGLISH TEACHER:**

*(Laughing)* And who could you possibly be? Don't try to show your violent nature here because I am crazier than you are.

**MR YAHYA NABIL:**

I can see you are in the mood for trouble and I am going to give you one surely.

**ENGLISH TEACHER:**

*(Laughing)* Of course! That is all that you people know. Suicide bombing and terrorism. But I swear that you can never bring those attitudes to my door steps. Don't even try it.

**MR YAHYA NABIL:**

*(He stares at him quietly)* Meet me in court *(He exits)*.

**ENGLISH TEACHER:**

*(Shouting behind him)* Which court? Do you know how many lawyers I know? *(To the audience)* I just hate these people and everything about them. I don't know why I agreed to talk with him in the first place *(He exits angrily and Narrator enters. She slowly paces the stage)*.

**NARRATOR:**

*(Sadly)* Why? Why? Why this open hatred for us and our Islam? What has Islam said that is wrong? Why must Islam go to court when a person by virtue of his Muslim name does something wrong? Why don't they hold their religion to task when a member of their religion does something wrong? Why must all Muslims be objects of ridicule for

one person's crime? Why have they chosen ignorance over knowledge? *(Hamida enters slowly)*.

**HAMIDA:**

As I walked, they called me names. Taliban, Osama Bin Laden, Terrorist, Al-Qaeda and many others. And they were tertiary students who should know better. They stand in front of my school Hall and insult him, the Prophet, the greatest man of all times. When I react, they call me violent.

**NARRATOR:**

It is like beating a child and forbidding him to cry. And they call us rowdy just because a few have been rowdy. But is rowdiness not found in every category of people? Whether Muslim or not?

**HAMIDA:**

To dodge these kinds of humiliations, most of us throw away the precious values that Islam instil in us and adopt the others. We want to be like everyone else. Very unfortunate! Very unfortunate.

**NARRATOR:**

Hmmm! Very very unfortunate indeed.

## A Letter to the Maker of Laws (A Stage Play)

**HAMIDA:**

Why don't they find out what Islam really is? Is the Qur'an not translated into the languages they understand? Are Hadith books and other Islamic literatures not all over the place in English? What is their fear? *(She exits)*

**NARRATOR:**

What is their fear? *(Lights go out and come on again with Hamida and Fatimatu Zahra seated on a mat)*

**HAMIDA:**

You know, these things must really be put to an end. When I was in the Senior High School, we the Muslims suffered a lot too and it is not different from what you are going through.

**FATIMATU ZAHRA:**

Sometimes, I really don't understand how some of them could hate us so much just because we are Muslims.

**HAMIDA:**

It is something that one can never fathom. You know the painful aspect forcing us to join them in their worship?

**FATIMATU ZAHRA:**

Tell me.

**HAMIDA:**

They say so many bad things about Islam that is so untrue that makes us cry sometimes. Because of that some would prefer to say they are not Muslims. It is a pity.

**FATIMATU ZAHRA:**

Things are no different now cousin. What I do is that when something like that happens, I walk up to the priest and try to explain what the truth really is to him.

**HAMIDA:**

*(Surprised)* You do that?

**FATIMATU ZAHRA:**

Yes, I do that.

**HAMIDA:**

And do they ever take it? They might turn you into an enemy one day.

**FATIMATU ZAHRA:**

*(She smiles)* The funny thing is that he always tends to apologise and blame his sources of information yet he never stops doing similar things. I'm trying to convince him to start reading the Qur'an and the ahaadith.

**HAMIDA:**

*(Impressed)* I always feel very proud of you cousin and I wish I had done what you are doing when I was like you but I know it is never too late.

## A Letter to the Maker of Laws (A Stage Play)

**FATIMATU ZAHRA:**

You are an inspiration to me sister and I love you very much.

**HAMIDA:**

I love you too a lot. *(Remembering something)* Aha! There was one thing I wanted you to include in your letter.

**FATIMATU ZAHRA:**

What is that? *(Lights go out and come on with Lawyer Musa sitting on a chair and Mma Safia Nurse on a mat)*

**LAWYER MUSA:**

I think we should take care of Hamida's nikah next week insha'a Allah and then we can end it with the court.

**MMA SAFIA NURSE:**

Yes, that is very true. Of late, most people meet me and they tell me that it sure looks like you are going to win this case for us.

**LAWYER MUSA:**

*(He laughs)* We will win the case insha'a Allah. I decided to become a lawyer because of some very basic and necessary human rights that people are deprived of for no concrete reason at all and Muslims are mostly part of these people.

**MMA SAFIA NURSE:**

*(She stares at him admiringly)* May Allah give us the blessings of our intentions and may He help us to achieve our objectives and goals in life.

Rubaba Mmahajia Rahma Sabtiu

**LAWYER MUSAH:**

Ameen. Ameen. Ameen. And may He guide us unto the path of righteousness and also make things easy for us.

**MMA SAFIA NURSE:**

Ameen thumma ameen. *(English Teacher comes through the door way)*

**ENGLISH TEACHER:**

*(Holding a bag)* Knocking!

**LAWYER MUSA:**

Come in *(He enters)*.

**ENGLISH TEACHER:**

*(Humbly)* Good afternoon Lawyer Musa.

**LAWYER MUSA:**

Good afternoon English Teacher.

**ENGLISH TEACHER:**

Good afternoon Mma Safia Nurse.

**MMA SAFIA NURSE:**

Good afternoon English Teacher.

**LAWYER MUSA:**

*(Pointing to a chair)* You may sit down.

## A Letter to the Maker of Laws (A Stage Play)

**ENGLISH TEACHER:**

Thank you very much Sir.

**MMA SAFIA NURSE:**

I think I would go inside.

**LAWYER MUSA:**

No, be here with us.

**MMA SAFIA NURSE:**

*(To English Teacher)* What may we offer you English Teacher?

**ENGLISH TEACHER:**

It is ok. I am very grateful.

**LAWYER MUSA:**

You don't do that in a Muslim home. At least, some water is ok.

**ENGLISH TEACHER:**

*(Smiling)* No problem then *(Fatimatu Zahra and Hamida enter hand-in-hand. Fatimatu Zahra is surprised to see English Teacher but they go to sit beside Mma Safia Nurse).*

**FATIMATU ZAHRA AND HAMDIA:**

May the peace, blessings and mercy of Allah be upon you *(They smile).*

**LAWYER MUSA AND MMA SAFIA NURSE:**

Same to you.

**LAWYER MUSA:**

*(Continues)* My modern ladies. *(At English Teacher)* You didn't respond.

**ENGLISH TEACHER:**

*(Smiling)* I didn't know how to respond to that else I would have.

**MMA SAFIA NURSE:**

Ok! That is acceptable. You need to learn.

**ENGLISH TEACHER:**

How are you Fatimatu Zahra?

**FATIMATU ZAHRA:**

*(Shyly)* I am fine and you?

**ENGLISH TEACHER:**

I am ok.

**MMA SAFIA NURSE:**

*(Happily staring at her daughter and Hamida)* Just look at these two birds of the same feathers.

**HAMIDA:**

Oh Auntie! You're just so sweet.

**LAWYER MUSA:**

Mmmm! Sweeter than me?

**HAMIDA:**

*(She pretends to be thinking)* Ehm! Zahra, what do you think?

## A Letter to the Maker of Laws (A Stage Play)

**FATIMATU ZAHRA:**

*(Smiling. She looks at her dad and then her mum)* Ehm! Ehm!

**LAWYER MUSA:**

*(Pretending to be surprised)* I thought it was going to be the easiest question ever sweetheart.

**MMA SAFIA NURSE:**

*(Excited)* You think so my husband? Mind you, you do have an able and a competitive competitor of a wife you know.

**LAWYER MUSAH:**

Ok! But Fati, you haven't answered my question.

**FATIMATU ZAHRA:**

You know what daddy. My sweet cousin asked the easiest question which is the most difficult to answer. *(They all laugh)* Let us not also forget that she was the one who was supposed to answer the question in the first place.

**HAMIDA:**

Ok! It looks like you people are busy. Come on lovely one! Let's go and work the question out. We will bring you an answer later *(They stand up and walk out as they all laugh)*.

**LAWYER MUSA:**

*(Still laughing)* I am very sorry English Teacher. These two girls are a fun most of the time and they mean the world to me.

**MMA SAFIA NURSE:**

(*Laughing*) Rightly said. We are very very sorry.

**ENGLISH TEACHER:**

Oh! It is all right. I like all that I saw.

**LAWYER MUSA:**

Good. By the way, how may we help you?

**ENGLISH TEACHER:**

I wanted you to do me a very great favour that I don't think I deserve.

**LAWYER MUSA:**

What kind of favour is that?

**ENGLISH TEACHER:**

I got into trouble with Mr Nabil Yahya and I thought that perhaps you could help me.

**LAWYER MUSA:**

What trouble is that and how do we help you?

**ENGLISH TEACHER:**

He came to me one time to talk to me about an issue and I was not so nice to him.

**LAWYER MUSA:**

Nice?

**ENGLISH TEACHER:**

I didn't know who he was then.

## A Letter to the Maker of Laws (A Stage Play)

**MMA SAFIA NURSE**:

You haven't answered the question. How were you not nice to him?

**ENGLISH TEACHER:**

I said some rude words to him.

**LAWYER MUSA:**

We know the entire story so stop beating about the bush. Would Nabil send you to court just because of some rude words you said to him?

**ENGLISH TEACHER:**

I actually, you know…

**MMA SAFIA NURSE**:

Why do you take pleasure in making the lives of those Muslim little ones so miserable?

**ENGLISH TEACHER:**

I am really sorry.

**LAWYER MUSA:**

I wanted to lock you up myself but I only took solace in my daughter's words.

**ENGLISH TEACHER:**

I swear, I am very sorry.

**LAWYER MUSA:**

But why don't you go and talk to Nabil himself?

**ENGLISH TEACHER:**

I went to his house but the security men would not allow me in and I went to your brother's house too but the same thing happened.

**MMA SAFIA NURSE:**

And what did you do to make the security men to allow you into our house?

**ENGLISH TEACHER:**

I told them I was Fatimatu Zahra's teacher and they cross-checked and found out that it was true.

**LAWYER MUSA:**

When you came to this house, did it look like we are a bunch of uncivilised people and terrorists? *(English Teacher is quiet).*

**MMA SAFIA NURSE:**

You have to be very careful with your dealings. You will never know where it will lead you.

**LAWYER MUSA:**

How do you need our help?

**ENGLISH TEACHER:**

The Board of the school is threatening to report me to the GES before they get into any trouble and the Muslim students with their non-Muslim friends and even some of the teachers are willing to prove to the court that…

# A Letter to the Maker of Laws (A Stage Play)

**MMA SAFIA NURSE:**

That what? *(He's quiet)*

**LAWYER MUSA:**

Nabil just came to settle permanently in this country and he is getting married to my niece Hamida just next week. You never had an idea whom he was or what he meant to the world. Did you ever ask him how he even got to know you and what you do to your students in school?

**ENGLISH TEACHER:**

No, I didn't.

**LAWYER MUSA:**

But you went ahead and proved to him that what he had heard was true and I can promise you that if you don't find a way of stopping him, he will make your life miserable as you deserve.

**ENGLISH TEACHER**:

*(Scared)* Oh Lawyer Musa! Please help me! I really don't want shame for myself and my family.

**MMA SAFIA NURSE:**

He is not going to lie against you. That man is a peace maker but he wanted to give you peace and you said no. Now he wants to send you to court for you to defend yourself and you don't want that either.

**LAWYER MUSA:**

He is not going to harm you in any way as you might be thinking because to you all Muslims are rowdy and violent. You will only face the court which you deem civilised and well organised.

**ENGLISH TEACHER:**

*(Disturbed)* You know, I was really ignorant about Islam and Muslims. The only thing I do is to always look for the bad things they say about Islam on the internet and other media and that gave me a very bad picture of Islam. About two weeks ago, after Mr. Nabil's visit, I received a parcel through my postal address. It contained an English translation of the Qur'an, a book about the traditions of the prophet and some others. I was so furious I nearly got them burnt right away until I saw a letter addressed to me in it. It was entitled, "Letter to the English Teacher" and it had the subtitle, "What do you know about Islam?" I was touched but I still wanted to burn it anyway. In the end, I decided to read it. *(He stops)*

**MMA SAFIA NURSE:**

*(Surprised)* Hmmm!

**LAWYER MUSA:**

Continue.

**ENGLISH TEACHER:**

# A Letter to the Maker of Laws (A Stage Play)

*(He looks down)* I cried throughout that day and I even fell sick. From then, I knew I had to change because I have been ignorant for far too long and I regret so much how I had caused so many Muslims so much pain and some in order to please me had denounced Islam.

**MMA SAFIA NURSE:**

Hmmm!

**LAWYER MUSAH:**

*(Sadly)* Was it Nabil who sent you the parcel?

**ENGLISH TEACHER:**

*(Quiet for a while)* That was what I thought at first but I was wrong. It was Fatimatu Zahra *(They are both surprised)*.

**MMA SAFIA NURSE:**

Subhaanal Laah! Subhaanal Laah!

**LAWYER MUSA:**

*(Tears in his eyes)* Oh Allah! Which of the favours You have bestowed upon me would I deny? My little girl. My blessing. Alhamdu lil Laah for our daughter.

**ENGLISH TEACHER:**

I showed the letter to my friends who also had these negative perceptions about Islam I did and you wouldn't believe it. They felt so ashamed of themselves and we have all decided to make photocopies of the letter and distribute it to people who are ignorant of Islam like us.

Rubaba Mmahajia Rahma Sabtiu

**MMA SAFIA NURSE:**

Allahu Akbar!

**LAWYER MUSA:**

Hmmm!

**ENGLISH TEACHER:**

*(He opens his bag and brings out a paper)* Here is the letter. I thought I should let you see it *(He gives it to Lawyer Musa).*

**LAWYER MUSA:**

*(He stares at it for a while and shakes his head. He hands it over to his wife)* Safia, please read it to us.

**MMA SAFIA NURSE:**

Hmmm! *(She also stares at the paper and they become motionless as Fatimatu Zahra's voice is heard in the background.)*

**FATIMATU ZAHRA:**

Hello English Teacher,

Forgive me for my informality and for sending you an English Qur'an and other Islamic books in English. Please don't throw them away. At least, finish reading this before you decide.

I always wonder and I keep asking myself, "Why does my English Teacher hate Islam so much?" I know you don't hate me but you hate my Islam for if I wasn't a Muslim,

44

perhaps I would have been one of your most beloved students. This also makes me ask, "What does my English Teacher hate about Islam?" I never find answers to them because even at my age, I could tell that even if you are not a Muslim, you can't help but admire Islam provided you know what it is.

I try hard day by day to find reasons not to hate you because you hated what I loved most. I tell myself, "Perhaps he doesn't know Islam." Then I tell myself again, "But why doesn't he take the pain to find out instead of holding unto misconceptions?" Then I tell myself again, "Perhaps he never had the chance to know the real truth about Islam." I battle within myself not to hate you even though you hated me and my Muslim brothers and sisters.

Indeed, I know and I believe that ignorance of anything in this century is unpardonable yet I try to give you the benefit of the doubt. Sometimes I want to ask, "Sir, please, is it because of the way Muslims worship that you hate us?" Then I imagine you say yes to this. Then in my dreams I try to explain that we do not worship any visible God and I feel like telling you the meanings of the things we say in all our acts of worship *(She pauses and the Narrator enters quietly)*.

**NARRATOR:**

Subhaanal Laah! Subhaanal Laah! Subhaanal Laah! Glorified be Allah above all that is in the Heavens and the Earth. *(To the audience)* Did you hear what I heard? Did you understand? Do you believe she could have written all that? Subhaanal Laah! Such a blazing passion *(She exits slowly and they come into motion. They all shake their heads in wonder).*

**MMA SAFIA NURSE:**

Allahu Akbar! Allahu Akbar! Allahu Akbar!

**LAWYER MUSA:**

Laa ilaaha illal Laah!

**ENGLISH TEACHER:**

Hmmm! There is more so just pay attention *(They become motionless and Fatimatu Zahra's voice is heard from the background again).*

**FATIMATU ZAHRA:**

I ask again, "Is it because of the way the females dress?" Then I want to tell you the essence of it. It is not to oppress me or any Muslim lady but to make us free women and to shield us from the illicit pleasures of men. I also feel like giving you reasons and prove that would more than convince you that indeed, a covered woman is far better than a nude woman.

The Muslim man and woman are equal in spirituality. I sometimes wonder how you understand the word Jihad and why you relate it to terrorism and holy wars and all the other bad things. Couldn't you find out what Jihad meant to the Muslim?

I think about how you could paint polygamy in Islam so black. You make it look as if it is without rules and significance and I wish I could explain to you the logic behind it.

## A Letter to the Maker of Laws (A Stage Play)

Something you can never deny is very beneficial when played by the rules *(She pauses and Kramo enters. He tries to make out where the voice is coming from and then he suddenly becomes motionless and Fatimatu Zahra's voice is heard in the background again)* Oh Sir! I have so many things to say yet I keep asking myself, "Would my first word be read? Would he be patient enough to read up to the end? Well, I tell myself, "I can only try my best." But if ever you are patient enough to read up to the end, I would plead with you to read the Qur'an and the other books and search for more information on Islam. This is not to make you a Muslim but to make you understand Islam which would help in maintaining peace between and among us. The hatred would not lead us anywhere except to destruction.

I apologise if I did or said anything you didn't like but what I know is that we can be different and still be at peace. Do not hate me because I do not want to hate you.

For nothing but peace!!!

Your humble student

Fatimatu Zahra Bint Musa *(Kramo comes into motion).*

**KRAMO:**

*(Surprised)* Who is talking? Is Fatimatu Zahra dead? Oh Master! You didn't do well at all. You didn't do well at all Master! *(He sits on the floor and begins to cry)*

**LAWYER MUSA:**

*(Confused, he stares at Kramo)* What's going on Kramo? *(He continues to cry)*

**MMA SAFIA NURSE:**

(Also confused) Kramo, is there any problem?

**KRAMO:**

(He stands up and he removes a big napkin from his pocket. He begins to wipe his face) Master, you didn't do well. You didn't do well master. You didn't tell me that Fatimatu has become a ghost (They all begin to laugh).

**LAWYER MUSA:**

Why do you think she has become a ghost?

**KRAMO:**

(He stares at them in surprise) Master and Master's wife, why are you laughing? Don't you know that your daughter is dead? (They continue to laugh)

**MMA SAFIA NURSE:**

You know what Kramo, I left you a sumptuous meal in the kitchen. Go and take care of yourself (Fatimatu Zahra enters).

**FATIMATU ZAHRA:**

(Walking towards Kramo excitedly) Where have you been Mr K?

**KRAMO:**

(He turns to the other side and strains his ears with his eyes wide opened) Master! (He goes to put his hand on Lawyer Musa's shoulder) Master! Can't you hear what I am hearing?

# A Letter to the Maker of Laws (A Stage Play)

**FATIMATU ZAHRA:**

*(Confused)* Mr K, sweet cousin wants to eat your food.

**KRAMO:**

*(He begins to run out)* My food! My food! *(He exits and they all laugh)*

**LAWYER MUSA:**

Come over here Fati *(She goes to sit beside her mother on the mat)* We are very proud of you.

**MMA SAFIA NURSE:**

Hmmm! You can never guess how much *(Lights go out on stage and come on with Fatimatu Zahra sitting by the desk).*

**FATIMATU ZAHRA:**

*(She writes)* The letter to my English Teacher did the magic and I thank Allah for the favour. But oh Maker of Laws! I keep asking myself, "Would my letter to you make a similar impact?" I want to say yes but who guarantees me that because I do not know that which is hidden. Another of my headaches is... *(Lights go out and come on with Kramo talking angrily).*

**KRAMO:**

*(Walking to and fro)* He insulted me! Oh God! He insulted me! *(He sits on the floor and begins to cry)* He insulted me! *(He stops crying)* But me, am I a dirty man? Why did he say that to me? *(Fatimatu Zahra enters).*

**FATIMATU ZAHRA:**

*(Happily)* Assalaamu alaikum Mr K.

**KRAMO:**

*(He turns to her)* He insulted me. Wa alaikum salaam. Fatimatu, the man insulted me.

**FATIMATU ZAHRA:**

Please stand up from the floor. *(He does)* Who insulted you?

**KRAMO:**

Aha! Would you write it?

**FATIMATU ZAHRA:**

Write what?

**KRAMO:**

The insult and me

**FATIMATU ZAHRA:**

Where would I write it?

**KRAMO:**

But that thing you are always writing. I want you to write my insult and my name inside.

**FATIMATU ZAHRA:**

Why?

# A Letter to the Maker of Laws (A Stage Play)

**KRAMO:**

But you write everyone's name in it.

**FATIMATU ZAHRA:**

*(Laughing)* Ok! What is the problem?

**KRAMO:**

*(Sadly)* I was coming and he was going and then she was following him and shouting.

Then I wanted to help her but he started insulting me.

**FATIMATU ZAHRA:**

*(Suppressing her laughter)* Let me see; a man came passing by and a lady was shouting at

him because of something then you try to help the lady and the trouble began.

**KRAMO:**

*(Laughing)* Yes! Yes! You are very good.

**FATIMATU ZAHRA:**

*(Calmly)* Where were you and why did you decide to help the lady?

**KRAMO:**

*(Quiet for a while)* I want to ask you a question.

**FATIMATU ZAHRA:**

I am listening.

**KRAMO:**

A nurse and a lawyer, which one do you want to become?

**FATIMATU ZAHRA:**

None. But why did you ask me that question?

**KRAMO:**

You are always asking me too many questions.

**FATIMATU ZAHRA:**

*(Smiling)* Oh! Is that so? But you don't answer them.

**KRAMO:**

I can't answer all of them because they are too difficult for me.

**FATIMATU ZAHRA:**

Ok. Just answer this one. Where were you and why did you decide to help that lady?

**KRAMO:**

*(As he is about to speak, he strains his ears to listen to something and they hear the Adhan in the background)* I am going to the Masjid. Bye bye! *(He runs out. She shakes her head and lights go out and come on with her sitting by the desk).*

**FATIMATU ZAHRA:**

*(She writes)* Indeed, Mr. Kramo is a very funny man and interesting to be with but even he is not free from the abusive words used against Muslims for the sake of Islam. Though he just accepted Islam, every little thing he does due to his culture is attributed to Islam and he is called names. Minor is this issue yet it is one of the numerous problems. And so many more I have yet to say but are these not enough of a headache?

## A Letter to the Maker of Laws (A Stage Play)

And Oh! My English Teacher… *(Lights go out and come on with Lawyer Musa and Mr. Yahya Nabil seated on a prayer mat, Mma Safia Nurse and Hamida also sit on another prayer mat and English Teacher sits on a chair near them)*

**LAWYER MUSA:**

*(To Mr. Yahya Nabil)* I'm telling you, he has learnt his lessons. I would have been the first to be partner with you in this. Please forgive him for the sake of Allah.

**MMA SAFIA NURSE:**

Please forgive him. The letter of a little girl was enough to make him see reason. Pardon him for now.

**ENGLISH TEACHER:**

*(He goes on his knees)* I am pleading with you to save me from this shame. I promise you that I now understand Islam better and I would not dare do any of those barbaric things I used to do. Please listen to my plea.

**MR YAHYA NABIL:**

*(Calmly)* Stand up. You don't have to kneel before me. You are forgiven totally but if I hear of any of those things again, you will surely not be spared of justice *(They become motionless and the Narrator enters).*

**NARRATOR:**

*(To the audience)* He is forgiven. He will always be forgiven and they will always be forgiven. Muslims must forgive because they never despair of the mercy of Allah *(She exits and lights go out on stage and come on with Fatimatu Zahra by the desk).*

Rubaba Mmahajia Rahma Sabtiu

**FATIMATU ZAHRA:**

They must all get one and insha'a Allah, they will all get one. *(Hamida enters and Fatimatu Zahra sees her)* Hey! See who is here.

**HAMIDA:**

Are you done with the list sweet one?

**FATIMATU ZAHRA:**

No, I am not. Could you help me out with it?

**HAMIDA:**

Sure, why not? Two good heads are better than one. Kramo would bring the envelopes and the letters soon.

**FATIMATU ZAHRA:**

*(Surprised)* You gave it to him? That is risky. I hope it gets here.

**HAMIDA:**

*(Laughing)* He collected it that he will give it to uncle himself.

**FATIMATU ZAHRA:**

And you let him?

**HAMIDA:**

When I got to the hall, both Kramo and uncle were there but Kramo wanted to put the letter in uncle's hand instead of me. Could you guess why?

## A Letter to the Maker of Laws (A Stage Play)

**FATIMATU ZAHRA:**

*(Laughing)* No.

**HAMIDA:**

He wants some of the reward from Allah

**FATIMATU ZAHRA:**

*(She laughs loudly)* This man is something else.

**HAMIDA:**

He said he would wait for uncle to finish photocopying it and then he will bring them *(They both laugh)*.

**FATIMATU ZAHRA:**

I wish him a save journey from daddy's office to the study and may Allah protect the letters and the envelopes.

**HAMIDA:**

Ameen thumma ameen. A less than one minute journey with such massive prayer, I am sure Allah will answer *(Lawyer Musa and Kramo enter with papers in their hands. They stare at them)*.

**KRAMO:**

You see. I brought the letters.

**LAWYER MUSA:**

He has the envelopes and I decided to escort him with the letters *(They all laugh except Kramo)*.

**FATIMATU ZAHRA:**

Well done, Mr. K *(She collects the envelopes).*

**HAMIDA:**

Thanks uncle *(She collects the letters).*

**LAWYER MUSA:**

You are welcome dear. *(They laugh and he points to Kramo)* I think you will need his help *(He exits and Fatimatu Zahra and Hamida go to sit on a mat on the floor. Kramo pulls a chair from the desk and sits near them).*

**KRAMO:**

How can I help you?

**FATIMATU ZAHRA:**

Wait…

**HAMIDA:**

I think we have about thirty copies of the letter. Who should we address it to first?

**FATIMATU ZAHRA:**

Why not write the list before?

**HAMIDA:**

Good idea *(She picks a pen and a paper)* I am ready?

**KRAMO:**

To the world and me.

## A Letter to the Maker of Laws (A Stage Play)

**FATIMATU ZAHRA:**

Great Mr K. Sweet one, let's address it to the world at large, the various continents, the countries in them, the regions, the districts and towns.

**HAMIDA:**

*(Writing)* That makes it complete. I think we need a lot more copies.

**FATIMATU ZAHRA:**

Daddy will take care of that.

**KRAMO:**

Then, this house will be full of letters. What about me? Won't you give me one?

**HAMIDA:**

*(She thinks for a while)* You know what? I think every individual must have the letter.

**FATIMATU ZAHRA:**

That is very true *(She is quiet for a while)*. But our target is not everybody but the Maker of Laws.

**KRAMO:**

*(He stands up)* I am not a Maker of Laws. Peace be with you.

**FATIMATU ZAHRA AND HAMIDA:**

*(Laughing)* And also with you *(He exits)*.

**HAMIDA:**

It is very necessary that we get it to the Maker of worldly laws first and then we can think of others besides them.

**FATIMATU ZAHRA:**

The question then is; "Who is the real Maker of laws?"

**HAMIDA:**

*(She stands up)* I think it is about time we make use of the lawyer in our home. Let's go and see uncle *(Fatimatu Zahra stands up. They take all the papers and exit. The Narrator enters quietly)*

**NARRATOR:**

Indeed, each one of us is a maker of laws in his or her own right. But! But! Who are the real Makers of laws? *(She pauses)* Many answers pop up in my head yet I dare not utter them. Afraid? Of course not! But the problem is, so many will agree with me and so many will disagree with me *(Mma Safia Nurse enters. She stands opposite the Narrator).*

**MMA SAFIA NURSE:**

*(She heaves a sigh)* I've had a day. Let me have some rest.

**NARRATOR:**

*(Just as she was about to sit on the mat)* Salaam to you Mma Safia Nurse.

**MMA SAFIA NURSE:**

Wa alaikis salaam Madam Storyteller. I didn't see you at first.

## A Letter to the Maker of Laws (A Stage Play)

**NARRATOR:**

Never mind. I know how tedious your job is. Your reward is only with our Creator. A thought just crossed my mind. Did your most precious daughter ever complete her letter?

**MMA SAFIA NURSE:**

You have indeed asked a question but I am yet to know that. But I think you should know best *(Lawyer Musa enters looking very exhausted)*.

**LAWYER MUSA:**

*(He stares at both the Narrator and his wife)* Salaam to you!

**BOTH:**

Wa alaikumus salaam.

**MMA SAFIA NURSE:**

You look exhausted. I thought today was your day off?

**LAWYER MUSA:**

I was hired by my daughter and my niece. A lucky man I have been today *(They laugh)*.

**NARRATOR:**

Lawyer Musa, may I ask you a question?

**LAWYER MUSA:**

Yes, you may Madam Storyteller.

**NARRATOR:**

Do you have any idea how your daughter ended her letter?

**LAWYER MUSA:**

*(He's quiet for a while)* Yes, I have.

**NARRATOR:**

I very much want to know.

**LAWYER MUSA:**

She blamed herself, me *(He points to himself)*, you *(He points to the Narrator)*, her *(He points to his wife)* and them *(He points to the audience)* for everything that she has always worried about.

**NARRATOR:**

*(Nodding)* I guessed right. Are the letters delivered yet?

**LAWYER MUSA:**

No, they are not. But every other thing is done *(Hamida enters looking exhausted as well)*.

**HAMIDA:**

*(She heaves a sigh and she looks around)* Hmmm! The story has almost come to an end. *(She smiles)* Salaam to you all.

**ALL:**

Wa alaikumus salaam *(They all stare at her)*.

**HAMIDA:**

*(Looking at them)* What is going on here?

# A Letter to the Maker of Laws (A Stage Play)

**MMA SAFIA NURSE:**

We were talking about Zahra's letter and how it ended.

**HAMIDA:**

*(As she is about to speak, English Teacher and Patrick enter)* Oh! We seem to have visitors

*(The Narrator leaves the stage unnoticed).*

**ENGLISH TEACHER AND PATRICK:**

Good evening

**ALL:**

Good evening

**LAWYER MUSA:**

*(To English Teacher)* How are you?

**ENGLISH TEACHER:**

I am doing great. *(He pauses as they stare at him)* I was coming with Patrick who has been helping me with the distribution of the letters to tell you about our success story so far when we met Mr. Yahya Nabil and he came to drop us.

**LAWYER MUSA:**

That is nice. Where is he?

**ENGLISH TEACHER:**

He is parking his car at the garage.

**MMA SAFIA NURSE:**

I think we should all sit down. Hamida, please get us something to sit on *(She exits and Nabil enters. He happily goes to hug Lawyer Musa)*

**MR. YAHYA NABIL:**

Assalaamu alaikum to you all.

**ALL EXCEPT ENGLISH TEACHER AND PATRICK:**

Wa alaikum salaam.

**MR. YAHYA NABIL:**

*(To Mma Safia Nurse)* O aunt Safia! You are making my uncle grow very tough *(They laugh and Hamida and Kramo enter with Hamida holding prayer mats and Kramo carrying chairs).*

**KRAMO:**

*(He puts the chairs down and rushes to hug Mr. Yahya Nabil)* I am too happy to see you Mr. Yahya. I hope you brought my Qur'an and Jalbab? *(Hamida spreads the mats).*

**MR. YAHYA NABIL:**

*(Laughing)* I did. And I added some other things that you would love.

**KRAMO:**

*(He goes back to bring the chairs)* I am very glad Mr. Yahya *(Kramo and Patrick sit on the chair, Mr. Yahya Nabil and English Teacher sit on one mat and Mma Safia Nurse and Hamida sit on another mat).*

## A Letter to the Maker of Laws (A Stage Play)

**LAWYER MUSA:**

*(Pulling a chair to sit on)* I like to have lots of people in the house. We look like a very big family.

**MMA SAFIA NURSE:**

*(Laughing)* It gives a whole new feeling.

**MR. YAHYA NABIL:**

Where is Fatimatu Zahra? Isn't she done with the letter?

**LAWYER MUSA:**

I think Mrs. Nabil also known as Personal Advisor De Fatimatu Zahra should answer that *(They all laugh)*.

**MR. YAHYA NABIL:**

*(Smiling)* Ok then, wife, the ball is in your court.

**HAMIDA:**

The precious Zahra is in the study doing a few things but she would be here soon. Her letter is done *(The Narrator enters and they all become motionless. She quietly goes to the front of the stage)*.

**NARRATOR:**

That intelligent and beautiful letter has ended. In her conclusion, she blamed herself and all of us for all that she thought wise to complain about *(She pauses and they come into motion. Kramo laughs loudly and everyone is surprised)*.

**KRAMO:**

*(He stands up happily)* My name is in the letter. She showed it to me *(The all laugh and they become motionless again)*.

**NARRATOR:**

*(Shaking her head)* All of us are in that precious letter. *(She pauses)* What were the words? What were the words she used in her conclusion? *(She exits and they come into motion)*.

**HAMIDA:**

*(She comes to the front of the stage and they all watch her)* In the conclusion of her letter she said… *(They become motionless and Fatimatu Zahra's voice is heard in the background)*

**FATIMATU ZAHRA:**

Oh Maker of laws! The list of complains is endless. Some of the problems cannot be solved even by your laws yet some can be instantly solved by a law that is fair to the Muslim woman and her career especially and all Muslims as a whole. I have blamed so many and I have a lot more to blame, starting with myself and every other Muslim.

One question holds some of us to blame is; "How do we present Islam to the corner of the world where we occupy?" Oh Maker of laws! Some of us Muslims have chosen to be in conflict with the rules of Islam yet some of us have chosen harmony with Islam. For the latter, I write this letter. We would indeed appreciate it if you bother enough to attend to our call as you owe us also a pledge and God indeed will bless you if you consider our appeal which is not harmful to any individual or society *(She enters the stage holding the letter with both hands and reading it as she walked)* What more can I say other than pray and wish that this letter reaches your favourable consideration. Forgive me once again if I have skipped protocol. All mistakes are mine. Thank you *(She smiles to all of them and they come into motion).*

**MMA SAFIA NURSE:**

*(Happily)* Marvelous! Subhaanal Laah!

**MR. YAHYA NABIL:**

This is worth all the millions in this world. Jazaakil Laah khair little one.

**HAMIDA:**

*(Laughing)* The girl is good. She is the best you could ever find.

**KRAMO:**

*(Mimicking Lawyer Musa who sits quietly with his head bowed. He gets up suddenly and then prostrate on the mat)* Allahu Akbar! *(He sits up).*

**ALL EXCEPT ENGLISH TEACHER AND PATRICK:**

Allahu Akbar!

**MR. YAHYA NABIL:**

This is too nice.

**KRAMO:**

Thank you Allah *(He goes to Fatimatu Zahra. Everyone stares at them).* Did I ever tell you?

**FATIMATU ZAHRA:**

*(Laughing)* What?

Rubaba Mmahajia Rahma Sabtiu

**KRAMO:**

You are good. You are very good. *(They all laugh)* And you are my youngest role model *(They become motionless).*

**FATIMATU ZAHRA:**

*(Coming into motion, she reads)*

Your worried citizen

Fatimatu Zahra Bint Musa *(She raises her head up, smiles and the Narrator enters)*

**NARRATOR:**

*(Looking at Fatimatu Zahra and smiling as she enters)* Well done! *(She turns to the audience)* She is worried and she is a citizen. She has a right to make an appeal to the movers of the economy where she belongs *(She exits and they all come into motion).*

**ENGLISH TEACHER:**

Honestly, I am totally lost of words.

**LAWYER MUSA:**

*(He stands up slowly and comes to the front of the stage)* If you were I, the father of this precious girl *(He points to his daughter)* or my wife *(He points to his wife)* or her cousin *(He points to his niece)* or any of these lovely people related to her somehow, what would you do to show appreciation to Allah for the good done you? *(He smiles and goes back to his seat. Fatimatu Zahra goes to sit beside Hamida).*

## A Letter to the Maker of Laws (A Stage Play)

**LAWYER MUSA:**

How are you Patrick?

**PATRICK:**

I am fine Sir.

**LAWYER MUSA:**

You are such a shy boy; you haven't uttered a word since.

**PATRICK:**

Sir, I am very happy to be here. Fatimatu Zahra has always thought me a lot.

**FATIMATU ZAHRA:**

*(Smiling)* Me? It is vice versa dad *(They laugh)*.

**MR. YAHYA NABIL:**

*(He makes a sign for everyone to pay attention)* I want my wife and I to take up the distribution of the letters and the follow ups as well.

**KRAMO:**

*(Sharply)* And me too Mr. Yahya.

**ENGLISH TEACHER:**

I think I would also love to do that for sure.

**PATRICK:**

*(Pleadingly)* Please, Mr. Nabil, I want to go with you.

**MMA SAFIA NURSE:**

Well, well, well. Nabil, what do you say to that?

**MR. YAHYA NABIL:**

I can see we all want to contribute. I was going to be selfish about it *(They become motionless).*

**FATIMATU ZAHRA:**

*(She stands up and starts pacing the stage)* You have done well. That is what they all say to me. Have I really done well? What makes them think so? A few words of appeal on a cheap piece of paper? What about those who did much more than that? The excitement must go down. There must be a response from those concerned first. A positive response *(The Narrator enters).*

**NARRATOR:**

And must the letter be distributed? For me it has been delivered. That was done when the last words were written. The echoes of those words of wisdom fill the air. Not even the Maker of laws will escape the strong force of its sound. And now I say; "There is no need for papers to be sent because a very little girl has already delivered the message to the world with her faint voice *(She exits and they come into motion again with each one of them doing his or her own thing).*

**KRAMO:**

Allah is great and good.

## A Letter to the Maker of Laws (A Stage Play)

**HAMIDA:**

*(Moving to the front of the stage, she starts singing)* Who made the clouds come by? So we can live and be, sending rain so soft and mild cleansing you and me?

**FATIMATU ZAHRA:**

*(Singing)* Who gave us clear eyes to see, the moon when it beams? He taught us how silent love can be, a road to our dreams.

**MR. YAHYA NABIL:**

*(Singing)* Who taught the mothers of the world, to love us the way they do? And as all the trials unfold, all they think of is us.

**MMA SAFIA NURSE:**

*(Singing)* You still make me cry. You still make us laugh. Don't let us ever forget, about our golden path.

**LAWYER MUSA:**

And so the world moves on its way. New comers join every day. Tomorrow they will say… Tomorrow they will say…

**KRAMO:**

That Fatimatu Zahra once wrote a very good letter *(They all laugh)*.

**ENGLISH TEACHER:**

That is very true. It is going to be history someday.

**PATRICK:**

Fatimatu Zahra will become very popular.

**LAWYER MUSA:**

I want to give each one of us a treat. I am making us a special lunch. Let's get to the sitting room *(They begin to stand up. Patrick goes to Fatimatu Zahra and talks silently to her as she laughs. English Teacher and Mr.*

*Yahya Nabil exit as they chat. Kramo says something to make Mma Safia Nurse laugh as they exit. Hamida and Lawyer Musa exit as Lawyer Musa says something to her. Patrick exits with Fatimatu Zahra and she comes back to the stage).*

**FATIMATU ZAHRA:**

*(She happily begins to fold the mats on the floor. She suddenly jumps out of joy)* I am happy. *(To the audience)* The maker of laws is going to listen *(She finishes folding them and puts them on the chair and walks slowly to one end of the stage and the Narrator enters through the other side of the stage).*

**NARRATOR:**

*(Staring at Fatimatu Zahra as she stares back. They both turn to the audience)* By the time!

**FATIMATU ZAHRA:**

Verily! Man is at a loss.

**NARRATOR:**

Except those who have believed.

**FATIMATU ZAHRA:**

And do righteous good deeds.

## A Letter to the Maker of Laws (A Stage Play)

**NARRATOR:**

And call one another to patience.

**FATIMATU ZAHRA:**

And call one another to the truth *(They pause and change positions)*.

**NARRATOR:**

The load is heavy. It is very heavy. One man, one woman, cannot carry the load. More hands are needed. She *(She points to Fatimatu Zahra)* just held her portion of the load. A great portion. What about you? What about you? *(She pauses)* What about me?

**FATIMATU ZAHRA:**

*(Surprised)* You? You have indeed held your portion by telling them what you tell them now and they have held their portion by lending listening ears to what you tell them *(Kramo enters)*.

**KRAMO:**

Fatimatu Zahra! Fatimatu Zahra! *(They turn to him. He looks at the Narrator shyly)* Assalaamu alaikum Madam Storyteller.

**NARRATOR:**

Wa alaikum salaam warahmatul Laah Kramo. How are you?

**KRAMO:**

Alhamdu lil Laah. Fatimatu Zahra, everyone is waiting for you *(She hurriedly goes for the mats and Kramo picks the chairs)*.

**FATIMATU ZAHRA:**

Let's go *(Kramo exits)*.

**NARRATOR:**

*(As Fatimatu Zahra is about to exit)* Stop! *(She stops and turns to her)* I am proud of you and the Muslim ummah are proud of you *(She smiles)*.

**FATIMATU ZAHRA:**

I am grateful. Alhamdu lil Laah. I am also proud of you and the Muslim ummah *(She laughs and exits)*.

**NARRATOR:**

*(Turning to the audience)* A just law is a basic requirement for any social structure. A just law guarantees the rights of all classes and individuals in accordance with the welfare of the public, accompanied by the implementation of its various codes. It is a natural law observed in all corners of the universe *(She pauses)*. They will listen! Insha'a Allah, it shall be done. Remember to look for a portion of the load to hold. Don't be only for yourself! Thank you. Assalaamu alaikum warahmatul Laah wabarkaatuh.

# THE END

# A Letter to the Maker of Laws (A Stage Play)

## GLOSSARY

| ARABIC WORDS | MEANING |
| --- | --- |
| Hijab | The dress code of the Muslim women |
| Insha'a Allah | If God wills |
| Eid | A day of celebration in Islam |
| Alhamdu lil Laah | All praise is due to Allah |
| Assalaamu alaikum | May peace be unto you |
| Wa rahmatul Laah | And the mercy of God |
| Wa barkaatuh | And His blessings |
| Wa alaikum salaam | And may peace be with you |
| Yaa | Oh! |
| Ahaadith | The sayings of the Prophet |
| Nikah | Marriage |
| Ameen | May it be so |
| Subhaanal Laah | Glorified is God above everything |
| Allahu Akbar | God is great |
| Laa ilaaha illal Laah | There is no god but God |
| Jihad | Striving against evil |
| Adhan | The call to the obligatory prayers |
| Salaam | Peace |
| Jalbab | An overall dress |

Rubaba Mmahajia Rahma Sabtiu

| | |
|---|---|
| Jazaakil Laahu khair | May God bless you with goodness |
| Ummah | People of the same believe |

# A Letter to the Maker of Laws (A Stage Play)